KEEP THE FEAST

KEEP *the* FEAST

POEMS

STEPHEN CUSHMAN

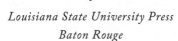

Louisiana State University Press
Baton Rouge

Publication of this book was made possible in part by funding from the Dean of Arts and Sciences and the Vice Provost for Research, University of Virginia.

Published by Louisiana State University Press
lsupress.org

LSU Press Paperback Original

DESIGNER: Michelle A. Neustrom
TYPEFACE: Adobe Caslon Pro

Cover illustration: *Still Life with Fruit, Oysters, and a Porcelain Bowl*, by Abraham Mignon (1660–1679), oil on panel. Courtesy the Rijksmuseum, purchased with the support of the Vereniging Rembrandt.

Grateful acknowledgment is made to the publications where the following poems first appeared: *About Place Journal:* "'Mary (Blind),' Stratford Hall"; *Alabama Literary Review:* "Bury a Body on Private Land," "Dark Social," "An Ether Purer," "Juicy Gossip," "Mated for Life," "The Progress of Railroading," and "Want to Make Something of It?"; *Beltway:* "Woman with the Arrow"; *Chronicle of Higher Education:* "List List" and "Time Management"; *The Concord Saunterer: A Journal of Thoreau Studies:* "He Chose Minnesota"; *The Ecopoetry Anthology:* "The Rain in Maine"; *Five Points:* "Charles Wright, Outside the Mailroom"; *Hampden-Sydney Poetry Review:* "Foreign Body" and "Single Origin Theory"; *Image:* "No Counting Sheep without Feeding Them Too," "The Fruit Thereof," and "Syllable Nutshell"; *Letters:* "Inserted in the Calendar"; *Literary Imagination:* "Perhaps One Sabbath" and "Woe to Us Hypocrites"; *Literary Matters:* "Dealey Plaza, November Again" and "Granny Was an Angelfish"; *Monticello in Mind: Fifty Contemporary Poems on Jefferson:* "Cut and Paste"; *More Truly and More Strange: 100 Contemporary Self-Portrait Poems:* "Love Your Neighbor as Your Self Portrait"; *Mountains Piled Upon Mountains: Appalachian Writing in the Anthropocene:* "Green Zebra," "Love in the Age of Inattention," and "No Historical Marker"; *Rappahannock Review:* "Peace and Quiet"; *The Recorder:* "I Am in Ireland Now'" and "May Contain Myth"; *Rome Review:* "Frequently Asked Questions"; *Smartish Pace:* "Crash Course" and "Crisis Hotline"; *South Carolina Review:* "Rommel's Option" and "We're Screwed"; *Southwest Review:* "Casserole for the Bereaved" and "The Qing Conquest Stirred Loyalist Passions"; *Streetlight:* "Accidental"; *32 Poems:* "Supposing Him to Be the Gardener"; and *Vindex:* "Rough Draft."

LIBRARY OF CONGRESS CATALOGING-IN-PUBLICATION DATA

Names: Cushman, Stephen, author.
Title: Keep the feast : poems / Stephen Cushman.
Description: Baton Rouge : Louisiana State University Press, [2022] | "LSU Press Paperback Original"
Identifiers: LCCN 2021055011 (print) | LCCN 2021055012 (ebook) | ISBN 978-0-8071-7494-4
  (paperback) | ISBN 978-0-8071-7805-8 (pdf) | ISBN 978-0-8071-7806-5 (epub)
Subjects: LCGFT: Poetry.
Classification: LCC PS3553.U745 K44 2022 (print) | LCC PS3553.U745 (ebook) | DDC 811/.54—dc23
LC record available at https://lccn.loc.gov/2021055011
LC ebook record available at https://lccn.loc.gov/2021055012

Contents

II.

III.

— I —

THE FRUIT THEREOF

Hold the phone, it wasn't an apple,
apples have seeds and seed-bearers, check,
perfectly fine in vegan Eden,
nor does the story name the fruit,
botanical paradox, fruit without seed,
which even those grapes, supposedly seedless,
have at some stage, albeit vestigial,
and if the tree delighted her eyes,
then Stevens was wrong, beauty in Eden
preceded death, the former the dam,
the latter her brat, aesthetic pleasure
in low-hanging stunners also permissible
and prelapsarian, given refraining
from touching or tasting, but just what sensation
followed her mouthful and subsequent double-take
at fresh sight of him, still oblivious
and suddenly scrumptious, for seconds or minutes
or panicky hours, if he proved stubborn,
unusually obtuse to all of her ogling,
the art of seduction not only fledgling
but lost on him too, immune to her itch

THE RAIN IN MAINE

fell also on the Etchemins, their name for us
humans, us builders of fish weirs,

us real people, as opposed to monsters,
animals, or the ghosts of others

back for a visit to glacial moraine
above the beach where clamming thrived

and the canoe route south could make good use
of easy portage across a bar

exposed at low tide, for which they also
must have had words, maybe one meaning

the waters inhale or the earth whale breaches,
as they would have had words for various arrowheads,

the kind meant for deer rather than seals
or for making war on trespassing tribes,

who bad as they were weren't so pathetic
as to need such abstractions

as religion, as nature, as beauty removed
from whatever gray weather the eagle glides through.

OVERNIGHT IN THE SHERFY HOUSE, GETTYSBURG

Would it be better to say the ghosts
came to a standstill beside the four-poster,
big eyes wide as dark socket
bullet holes in soft brick outside
upstairs bedroom facing the barn
burning them in it, came to stand close
at ease but in lines awaiting the word
Go forth and kill by apple and peach,
or would it be better to keep the slim peace
and say on the solstice these fields all turned
clear fields of fire at evening with fireflies,
even the shade trees, suddenly incendiary,
alight with small snipers blasting away,
most ever seen, and leave it at that?

LOVE IN THE AGE OF INATTENTION

What I like best about turning a corner
and seeing a snake, seeing me, coil
is having each other's complete attention.
Nobody saying, What were you were saying?
Neither not focused, eyes of both parties
never so locked. Could you hold, please?
That's not happening. Same goes for meeting
a deer, a hawk, a fox, a bear. Everybody stretched
thin toward the other. You prefer animals
because you fear intimacy, she said from the bed
and glanced at her phone.

LOVE YOUR NEIGHBOR AS YOUR SELF PORTRAIT

Twenty-four and blue's her favorite color,
All frequencies, wavelengths, nanometres, ångströms
From well-nigh green to in the violet ballpark,
Cerulescent, cyanean, azurine, trochaic terms
She's never used and hasn't told a soul today
There's no blue pigment in blue eyes
So why trust them, it goes to show, her own the brown
Of pumpernickel on the shelves of aisle fourteen
Not again till Monday, this is Sunday, her day to shop
Instead of church, she doesn't need a list, she knows she needs
A gallon of bleach in aisle twelve, there's lots to clean,
There always is, she even has a coupon for this kind
Labeled with that certain hue Vermeer would make
By crushing lapis lazuli, what do you call it, ultramarine
In lots of moods, woman in blue reading a letter,
Young woman with a water pitcher, lady seated at a virginal
Don't have much to do with aisle twelve, and yet they share a lot
With her of saturation, vividness, intensity, it must be grand
To study painting, know some things of shades and tints,
Wear a smock, have an easel, cultivate a personal palette,
Twenty-four, five foot two, scar on left cheek,
Blue her favorite color though she hardly wears it
And will not now, not anytime soon, twenty to thirty,
Held on bond, assigned an attorney, enter a plea
For grabbing that bastard by rarely washed hair
After he told her what others had too, treat me like that
Here's what you get, holding him down and pouring the bleach
Over his head, his once beloved face, too much down the throat
That tries to yell out the impolite words
Made harder to form by clear caustic substance.

TIME MANAGEMENT

Oil change: every three thousand;
tire rotation: every five thousand;
dental check-up: every six months;
annual physical: figure it out;
paint the house: one side a summer;
service the furnace: every October;
mow the grass: once a fortnight,
except in drought, if one's informal;
rake the leaves: easier to mow them;
turn over new leaf: every January;
shave the face: every other day
makes the shave closer;
brush the teeth: morning and evening;
floss the teeth: when stuff gets caught;
read the Bible: morning and evening;
reread *Walden:* in phases of crisis;
hug somebody: eleven times a day
for emotional health according to an article;
rejoice in being so bourgeois: once in a while
but only as needed; honor eros:
could be frequently, at least in theory;
serve eros: could be less frequently,
at least in practice; pray without ceasing:
figure it out; pump out the septic:
three to five years, easy to remember
with elections for president.

LIST LIST

Wine list, wish list,

to do list, top ten list,

grocery list, Christmas list,

price list, packing list,

bestseller list, mailing list,

back list, short list,

passenger list, casualty list,

guest list, shit list,

black list, hit list.

FREQUENTLY ASKED QUESTIONS

What time is it? How much does it cost?
Do spiders have dreams? Where are we going?
What difference does it make? Will this plane crash?
Why do you ask? Does that feel good?

What's Sanskrit for ecstasy? How long have I got?
Can you use it in a sentence? If it's high tide here,
is it low tide there? May I see your driver's license?
Where did you get such a ravishing rib cage?

Does life exist elsewhere? What's the point? Is it hard
to perform your own tracheotomy? Would you call a taxi?
Where's the bathroom? Is service included? Do you think
I look fat? What is prayer?

Got a light? White or red? Do you have this
in a larger size? What grade are you in?
Which way to Pisa? Why did I ever say yes?
Who is my neighbor? Business or pleasure?

Is this seat free? What's the local specialty?
Haven't we discussed disgust? Why have you forsaken me?
Does my vote count? What kind of bird was that?
Do they speak English? Am I hurting you?

Spare some change? Which way's north? Will you wait for me?
Think it'll snow? What does she want for her birthday?
Where's the nearest emergency exit? Will you take a check?
Is there stuff in my teeth? Faster or slower?

Have you seen my glasses? Do I need a reservation?
How do you spell that? Anything from the mini-bar?
What are you wearing? Does it help to fight back
when attacked by a mountain lion? Promise?

ROUGH DRAFT

Mark 8:24

No one always gets it right
Right off the bat, very first try,
Even if it's always worked
This way before, taking his hand
To guide him out through the gossipy village
Down to the lakeshore, a shady spot
For spitting into each arid eye,
Maybe too much or not enough
Saliva connecting with iris, pupil,
Cornea, tear duct, or was it spitting
From too far away or with one's own mouth
Slightly dry or in high wind that made him see
People at first as walking trees?

WE'RE SCREWED

If you're made in God's image
and the sun goes around
making in turn an image of you
each time it throws your darkness down
on sidewalk or doorstep take that
and that what the heck
are you to do
about keeping sacred
the second commandment

NO HISTORICAL MARKER

Pocosin Mission, Blue Ridge

Good Lord, Lord,
just what pit have we slipped into?
they could have whimpered, cringing in that cabin,
little more than lean-to, the Towles sisters,
Florence and Marion, Bishop-commissioned
into brute wilderness, ogres howling
blind with moonshine, she-wolves tight
with stunted superstition, bad luck to brush,
after baby's born, hair for nine days,
if baby has thrush, find a seventh child
to blow into its mouth, baby born at midnight
can see and talk to ghosts, good Lord, Lord,
two spinster missionaries must have been tough
to tough out an outpost thrown to the mountains,
nothing left of chapel walls but mossy rocks
and four green stairs to sing ascent
through frosty air, arise, shine, Christmas Day
again today, how could their way, native to Asia,
ever take hold where few people probed
farther from home than one day's ride,
kingdom of snakeroot, bloodroot, trillium,
if not for its weedy, expedient genius.

"MARY (BLIND)," STRATFORD HALL

Westmoreland County, Virginia

Eight years old and good as a bat,
clicking that tongue on the roof of her mouth
for echolocation, bed, table, chair,
no problem for her in Nelly's small cabin
whenever she moved to the fireplace sniffing
while scanning low flames with skin wide-eyed
to lift a hot pot off, wholly unknowing
she had no value, zeroes by her name
in the '82 inventory.

THE PROGRESS OF RAILROADING

Union Station, Washington, DC

The one with bare boob and wheatsheaf in lieu
of her usual scales, that would be Themis
without modern blindfold but still with a sword
and eighteen feet tall, FAIREST OF ALL
O FREEDOM, oracular, mother of Horae
by gigolo Zeus and paired with Apollo
above central arch for triumph through loggia
to vaulted white hall in gold leaf and granite
where twenty-six centurions, rumored as naked
behind their big shields, keep watch on travelers
and those going nowhere, one with a hand out,
shuffling, mumbling, too thin to hold up
pants that emancipate woe-to-you moon.

DEALEY PLAZA, NOVEMBER AGAIN

The live oak still lives in the birthplace of Dallas,
ramified high enough, fifty falls after,
to block a bead drawn from the sixth-story window
at Houston and Elm. Why call it story?
Says here originally a row of windows
painted with pictures, but what's the story
of a white-gloved hand grabbing the arm
that jerked up convulsed? What a day.
The sun crusades across the sky
despite the dark attacking early
as highs hit eighty, but does it count
as Indian summer without a prerequisite
killing frost? Doesn't say here
why Indian summer, and as for pictures
a thousand words each, no way
any picture snapped at the scene
ever beat *assassination*
lisped by a six-year-old
missing two teeth. What a day.
No wonder he wanted the top down.

AGAINST EROSION

Too much rain and dirt road gully
cuts even deeper, too little rain
or abstinent none and the creek disappears
uncovering bottom not quite the same
as uncovered yours, Apocalypso,
but trove all the same of muddy flat stones
to cobble the gully, slowly inset
moveable bed of ritual slowness
making it stately, each trip to the creek
for armloads of stones to charm the last *ion*,
while a thrush thrills, off our erosion.

HER NAME WAS COURAGE

Olga Rudge

No, not Atlantis; this is just Venice,
new moon, high tide, lagoon running over
a pooling piazza dotted with drains.

Back home the deer are getting much darker
now that it's legal to hunt them with bows,
but here the pursuer wells up through sewers
or breaks on the stairs of waterside walkways,
green smashed to spray and back-washing foam.
Places go under, sooner or later.

Back home, back home, it's time to go home
and lie with a loved one, assuming one has one,
but this is home also, or has been for some,
though you'd never know from guidebook direction,

Turning left here, note the façade, diagonally opposite,
or something of that sort, equally celibate,
façade duly noted, duly and dully

and both of them opposite to how she flowed home
when he graced the town, away from his wife,
across the arched bridge, along small canal
bobbing with workboats, then left at her street
to a black-green front door in pink plaster wall

where there's now a plaque, not to her
but to him, *mai spento amore,* never-spent love
for Venice, it says,

where she endures too,
first name and last, foreign and maiden,
engraved on a plate by a fisheye peephole

smack in the mouth of a bellowing lion.

CHARLES WRIGHT,
OUTSIDE THE MAILROOM

Come to think of it, I can think
of only one kiss in all your work,

which always sounds a lot to me
like nothing else in Tennessee,

and that's the *cold kiss of release*
in redemption, Bible camp, 1949;

yet, maestro, here you go
smacking your lips against a cheek

of mine, unshaven on my birthday,
because it's my birthday,

left, then right, Italian style,
the way no man would kiss another

in Pickwick Dam, at least in public
like this, your kiss

a slapstick joke, *solo uno scherzo,*
but a blessing witnessed nevertheless

and valued more for not having been
conned from you by a sheepskin swindle.

If only you'd asked him there in San Marco,
side by side, not so tongue-tied,

if only you'd managed to stutter through,
before he flew in '72,

Maestro mio, benedici anche me!
Pound might have done as much for you.

WOMAN WITH THE ARROW

Rembrandt, 1661

Without a union for working nude models
of northern Europe in the seventeenth century,
could they insist on no long sittings
except in summers or other warm spells?

Or maybe they came tougher then,
skin unshaved and rarely bathed
giving each woman more insulation,
which when combined with a fire nearby,
and her few extra pounds of calories stored up,
could make conditions almost cozy.

Sure, that's it. And if she's also
the master's mistress, no marathon session,
no matter how chilly before central heating,
consists of all work

posing in a yoga twist,
head going one way, torso another,
legs still another with a foot on the floor
at the edge of the bed and the arrow held up,
perhaps because arrows held toward the ceiling

enhance digestion or ward off bad dreams
or help one forget how cold the room feels

two years later when Hendrickje's dead,
he's widowed again, and all that remains
of her hips and buttocks, thighs and feet

acid incised in a copper plate
after the burin had stripped off her shape
from a ground of bitumen, beeswax, and resin.

WANT TO MAKE SOMETHING OF IT?

Matthew 21:18–22

Rain-sucking son of an acorn.
Photosynthesizing sack of sap.
Back off. You can spot a faith insufficient
to wither you like the fig tree cursed?
Care to risk it? Skipping breakfast makes one testy.
Especially on the road to town. Is that a dare?
I execrate your pollen-spewing. I abominate
your stumbling-roots. Bark-face. Leaf-bag.
Your xylem I anathematize. I'll make you wish
you had gone down in the weekend tornado.
I'll make you regret you excrete oxygen.
Add another ring? Don't make me laugh.
Say your prayers, arrogant angiosperm.
I'll teach your kind to mess with a teacher,
hungry and doomed, his last Monday morning.

INSERTED IN THE CALENDAR

Caravaggio, *Incredulità di san Tommaso*

Dactylon hōthe, digitum huc,
hither thy finger to feast in the gash
of unbroken black, poke the fat shadows
shafted with light in clear-dark baroque
it never quite is, no matter how badly
the sun has betrayed us, how faithless it's been
with hemispheres elsewhere, don't be so faithless,
put it right here, your pointer exactly
on where he gets off, suggestive Caravaggio
getting off somehow on slipping an index
into that slit, apocryphal, unbiblical,
what does it say, it says confession
but not penetration, in his whole oeuvre
no lady nude, what incredulity, hither the finger
adoring withholds from skeptical diddling,
what is believing but light enough to see
obscurity clearly, what better saint
for our shortest day, Wednesday this year,
over the hump.

BURY A BODY ON PRIVATE LAND

and you should draw a map of the site
and file it with the property deed
so the place will be clear to others to come
as it won't be in this case in two or three summers,
no casket or stone but just her soft mound
in the woods on a ridge above a thin creek
she studied through moods and most kinds of weather
as though she's snuggled under a quilt
in fetal position, her hip the high point.

SUPPOSING HIM TO BE THE GARDENER

Supposing this to be the sun
And this to be the rain,
Supposing clouds to be caviar
And wind to be champagne,

How can one tell divinity
From a tree turned red,
Or *Do not hold me* from what else
Its leaves might well have said?

NO COUNTING SHEEP WITHOUT
FEEDING THEM TOO

Sleeping pill dependence
may prompt referral
to laboratory overnights

(Polysomnography,
would you look good on me,
electrodes attached?),

and wee-hour waking may be a sign
of depression, it says,
but what could depress

when neither son of Zebedee
needed hypnotics, white ones like these
approved by the Air Force

in support of mission readiness,
to help them blow z's
through the garden where an oil press

explains the name Gethsemane,
where someone gone cold turkey
on this last night, before arrest,

could easily watch with thee.

SYLLABLE NUTSHELL

G is for onset,
kickoff, square one,
raging beginning
of in the beginning
out of the starting gate,
raw originality
in original sense,
and if consonantal
sine qua non
for vanity plates.

O is for nucleus,
sonorous meat
in a syllable sandwich,
bellybutton earful,
always a vowel,
animal imperative
enough in itself
to tell the whole story
of many a love,
oh ooh ah ow,
though not essential
for vanity plates.

D is for coda,
finishing touch,
all she wrote,
it's been real,
that's a wrap
and if consonantal
required reading

on vanity plates,
three parts, one syllable,
QED
a trinity.

— II —

Aflame are those whose way is austere,
      who walk in their ardors barefoot!
Aflame are those who thrive on restraint,
      who crave it without cessation,
who also do a little good
      now and then in spite of themselves!
Who has made the steadfast rules
      not even the lawless can break?
O that my ways may be rapturous
      in knuckling under those rules!
Then I shall not mope and pout,
      having endorphins always on high.
I will praise the way things go
      as I transmute them into euphorics.
I will observe small hints and signals;
      O lower not my pain threshold!

Beginners can usually keep their ways steady
        by freebasing steadiness into an ecstasy.
With my whole heart I seek to praise;
        let me not quibble what is praiseworthy!
I have laid up thy voice in my inner ear
        that I might not lose my tipsy balance.
Blessed be all chronic bummers;
        teach me to savor them more than strong wine.
With my lips I declare
        all the aptitudes of thy mouth.
In the way of thy lineaments I delight
        more than in all self-promotion.
I will meditate on thy topography
        and fix my eyes on thy kinesis.
I will exult in thy imperatives;
        I will not forget thy cries.

Commingle companionably with thy servant,
      that I might live a life and a half.
Upgrade my eyes that they may sustain
      appetite for appetite in the midst of disgust.
I am a temp on earth;
      hide not seniority's benefits from me!
My days are consumed with longing
      for longing to satisfy all by itself.
Do the insolent get rebuked
      for what to them was reverence?
Take from me scorn and venomous contempt,
      for both these things cause tachycardia.
Even though presidents can preside badly,
      thy servant will cherish all thy initiatives.
Thy policies are my delights,
      whether from thy left wing or thy right.

Drudgery cleaves to repetition;
    revive me when it depletes me!
When I confessed a weakness for pattern,
    thou didst bare thy patterns aplenty;
        bare some variations, too!
Make me flush for the artificial,
    but help me also insert the authentic.
Sometimes I sidetrack into an excess;
    give me thy hand, if not thy foot.
Put boredom far from me;
    and gently stimulate with thy requirements.
I have chosen the way of eagerness,
    although it comes from Latin for sharp.
I cleave to thy whetting, O Friction;
    let my bluntness not be dull!
I will try to keep from wilting
    as long as thou wilt hone.

Explicate, please, the skinny on beauty;
>   but don't expect me to keep it a secret.
Is it confined to sunsets and seashores,
>   to youthful vigor or fashioned enhancement?
Or does it exude from slow decline also,
>   as well as from cruelty and death-toll catastrophe?
Incline my heart, if there, to see it,
>   and not to finick with sugared aesthetics.
Turn my eyes from toying with trinkets;
>   and tutor me in beauty fiercer than baby food.
Don't let thy servant dismiss as monstrous
>   asking if beauty inhabits disaster.
Turn reproach away from the question;
>   for maybe my notions of beauty have blinded me.
Behold, I long for thy perspective;
>   in thy compassion forgive such longing.

Fetter my flailing limbs to thee,
      confining me with strict designs;
then shall I answer those who taunt
      that freedom precludes all fettering.
And take not the taste of thy warm truth utterly
   out of my mouth,
      though it chew a bud of clove.
I will invent new ways to please thee,
      as long as thou art receptive;
and I shall walk at liberty,
      for thy fantasies shackle me.
I will also speak of serving thee
      only in roundabout ways like this;
for I discover delight in thy service,
      which I happen to find satisfactory.
I revere all thy demands,
      and I will meditate on their specifics.

Grease my blues with heated oil,
        with all the ointment of thy immanence.
This is my lubricant in chafing scrapes,
        that inside thee is cresting continuous.
High achievers might think it slothful,
        but once enfolded I can sit still.
When I think of thy importunings,
        I take comfort, O Rippling Pressure.
Sometimes sadness seizes my throat
        for those who do not know thy touch.
That thou art tangible has been my song
        hummed off-key in numbing hours.
I remember thy nickname at night
        but speak it to no one, even in sleep.
This blessing has fallen to me,
        that I have had a taste of thee.

Hilarious eyesight has been my portion;
    I promise to believe in promise.
I entreat thy help for my poor nose,
    which doesn't really smell so well.
When I imagine thy emanations,
    I know I must be missing some.
I strain with my olfactory nerve
    to catch every essence of thy essence.
Though my nostrils are often obtuse,
    I do not forget those scents I catch.
At midnight I typically salivate
    because of thy righteous aromas.
I am devoted to thy exudings,
    to fumes and holy pheromones.
My world is full of thy redolence;
    teach me even more of thy odors!

Imbecility has cost thy servant,
  but so far I can afford it.
Teach me to act more sober when sober,
  for I have had some trouble doing so.
I used to think sobriety tiresome,
  but now I find it makes me giggle.
Sobriety's fun but also addictive;
  teach me how to avoid addiction.
Hipper spirits find me square,
  but among the square am I deviant?
Their hearts are about as average as mine,
  so I'm really grateful for thy favors.
I guess it's okay if I seem eccentric,
  though I have to admit I thought I wasn't.
I know I'm not central or even centered,
  but I thought at least I could pass for centrist,

juggling extremes as best I can,
>
> thanks to thy hands, which often steady,

though thou knowest me well enough

> to know that sometimes they also stir,

as does thy mouth whose laws are much better

> than thousands on paper in a bullish market!

Let me catch my breath a minute,

> for thinking of thee can be overwhelming.

Let thy servant abstain from debate

> with those who say they do not believe.

Let those who think thy lover naive

> rejoice in their skeptical worship of evidence.

Let thy lover always remember

> that believe and libido share the same root

with lover, quodlibet, beloved, and leman,

> so when I believe I believe in my leman

kissing thy servant with tongue in my mouth
        the moment these eyes open to light.
Forgive thy lover's unskillful arguments
        and total failure to come up with evidence
for having thy tongue so deep in his mouth
        or in his ear or so forth and so on.
For though I may be a wineskin in smoke,
        yet never have I forgotten thy tongue,
and when they say they do not believe,
        I'm perfectly happy to accept their testimonies
that each of their mouths houses one tongue,
        which need never tangle itself with another.
How could anyone convince of this intimacy
        those who insist they do not feel it,
especially those who are proud that they don't,
        especially those who call it superstition?

Lead me apart in paths of solitude
      where I can delight in keeping thee company.
Fortify thy servant with thy intensity,
      which doubles as a potent calmative.
Refresh me with heat that I may keep cool
      even when the blue jays pant.
I want to make thy lap guffaw
      with my own lap's infectious laughter.
I am thine, save me,
      though I know it's not thy job
to lavish attention on somebody else
      who doesn't lavish it on others
nearly as much as might be good for them
      or as much as they might like.
But I am thine even so;
      let me let saving take care of itself.

Most high on high, I love thy ankles!
They almost sprain my meditations.
Thy incarnations make my head swim
        now the breast stroke, now the back.
Infatuation has been my teacher;
        I do not mind the homework assigned.
I give thanks that few people care
        if I come out as an anthropomorphist.
I deny my devotion to no human trait,
        provided that trait takes flesh in thee.
I do not shun the animal either,
        for thou hast taught me.
How sweet thy teachings by light and by dark,
        even when they wound or bruise.
Through thy teachings comes much wondering
        who guards the border of pleasure and pain?

No wonder thy feet are lamps to my words
        and candles I hold when power cuts out.
I usually choose to eat no meat,
        but with thee the issue gets complex.
Cereals, grains, fruits, and greens,
        but then I turn to dine on thee.
Thy calves and knees wake me from sleep
        like someone shouting because of wine.
I am sorely afflicted with cannibal questions,
        and that's before I get to thy loins,
one more word that means many things,
        but as for a loincloth, the sky is thine.
Accept my praises when it lifts
        or divinest breezes blow it aside.
Incline the mouth that speaks in my heart
        to do whatever thy lips command

over and over till thou criest uncle
>   or aunt or cousin twice removed
or Ho! as in Zechariah, chapter two, verse six,
>   or whatever thou criest, if thou dost,
when theosexuals lose all perspective
>   on male and female, their mating choices,
who's rich, who's not, on epidermal pigmentation
>   and other markers at the mall
or in large traffic jams and junk food aisles,
>   priapic or estrual or both unbearably,
wanting thee because the plain
>   the bleak the drab the dreary the stale
the flat the vapid the soulless arouse
>   when worn by thee right next to the skin
to ensure thy servant's swooning or seizure.

Perhaps it should be deisexual
>to keep etymologies from intermarrying,
but theosexuals are on the same page,
>or would be if ever they were defined,
with Theravada and Saint Theresa;
>yet let me not be distracted from thee
by qualifications so far beyond me
>they mess up our indentation pattern.
Thou art my refuge, my roof, and my bed;
>thou art my altar, my window, my glasses.
Thou art my fire, my boot, my coat;
>thou art my water and my wine.
It is time for thee to act;
>indent me with thy gracious blank space.
My flesh trembles for thinking of thee;
>I do not fear my trembling ending.

Quasi-fervor could make thee queasy
    and faith faked could make thee upchuck.
Rescue me from pseudo-passion,
    and bathe me when I reek of heresy.
If beauty pleases through the sight
    or delights us through the sense of hearing,
what could beauty have to do
    with what, unseen, comes wholly hushed?
If no one sees thy face and lives,
    will bodily knowledge of thee annihilate?
I do not need more proof of thee.
    In fact, I don't need any.
I can't keep from breathing through my mouth
    when thy absence climbs aboard.
I cannot keep my blood from pounding
    when I do not hear thee growl.

Redeemer, Redeemer, Redeemer Supreme,
    please don't show me any more thigh,
albeit invisible, or bring it nigh
        through the slit in the skirt of thy world.
Too much rapture and I could expire
        even earlier than is expected.
Although I am petty and pretty selfish,
        thou canst slake me past all jealousy.
I do not mind if thou dost another.
        I do not mind if thou dost seven billion,
or if after us living thou turn'st to the dead
        and dost the billions on billions of them.
I truly desire this orgy for thee,
        if it would be thy will done.
But I do not think it will happen yet.
        Some won't stiffen; some won't wet.

Search me why I'm so loony for thee;
      maybe one day they'll find it's genetic.
I used to awake before dawn and cry why;
      I used to rend my boxers and brood.
Now before dawn I lie nude and review
      the scrumptious bluffs of thy blessed buttocks.
Do I blaspheme in praising those bluffs?
      Will the nonplussed take them as figurative?
I do not mean to seem obscene;
      what good is prayer that's only pornographic?
It's just that thy bluffs are literal to me;
      no mere metaphor moves as they do.
Moses glimpsed thee once from behind;
      he, too, knew this backside beatitude.
When one more failure threatens to turn
      joy to ash, thy butt is my but.

Thou, thee, thy, thine:
        teach me how to pronounce these pronouns
more often than *I, me, my, mine*
        and much could begin to begin to improve.
Must I accept what I cannot deny?
        One or the other without middle ground?
Keep me from seeking a happy medium
        in cases where happiness has nothing to do with it.
I do not deny that thou keep'st subtracting
        days from the number I have left to squander.
But do I have to accept that subtraction,
        since it proceeds, accepted or no?
Or is acceptance something received,
        a gift that thou givest if it should please thee?
Let me declare my love of thee
        doesn't depend on thine of me.

Unzip my vanity and slide it down slowly;
  strip off stuck-upness and toss it aside.
I rejoice at thy caress
  like a burn balmed with aloe.
I regret my weakness for notice
  and often wish I were invisible.
Seven times daily I turn to praise thee
  for making no fuss over me at all.
Great peace have those who love anonymity;
  nothing can make them perform or show off.
They do not restrain their hymns to thee
  with thoughts of what another might think.
They do not make small fools of themselves
  trying to make big names for themselves.
They do not idolize their own reputations
  or gorge themselves on the famine of fame.

Vouchsafe thy voluptuous curves to me,
      the curve of morning and afternoon,
the curve of evening and moonless night;
      vouchsafe to thy votary
a way to contain his tizzies and dithers
      without pretending others' ordeals
have nothing whatever to do with him
      and distant ailings aren't his problem.
Abstaining from news cuts down on drama
      but doesn't excuse from sharing affliction.
Give him bliss but soak it in brine
      to remind him of the privilege of bliss
and obligations it entails;
      let him exult so he can encourage.
He may stray like someone self-satisfied;
      save him from the complacent cesspit.

Whither can thy servant turn
    and not find thee there before him?
Whither can his eye revolve
    and not see dust thou art raising?
How can his ear, even if deaf,
    shut out the buzz of constant current
charging the wind with thy high voltage
    and effervescing through his bloodstream?
Behold, how doggedly days do their job
    and how the hours persevere!
Soon they will demolish thy servant
    and dismantle his worshipful voice.
If he should cover his head with ashes,
    pay him not the slightest mind.
Do not let him get away
    with some glib quip or facile finale.

Xerophilous means flourishing
    In a dry environment.
Whatever comes next or doesn't come ever,
    I thank thee for making me
xerophilous these many years,
    at least withstanding when flourishing faltered,
thanks to a fingertip wet by thy mouth
    before it traced a naked nipple.
Thy saliva wards off withering;
    irrigate with thy secretions!
O, Most High, I did not ask;
    in fact, I thought we were done for today.
But speaking this way now resuscitates,
    and I can manage a little longer!
Lead me in the path of commandments,
    in which I delight as long as I can

yell aloud with limbs yoked to thine,
       sitting or standing, prone or supine.
Why was I falling in love with the end?
       Why was I starting to work toward closure?
Thy eyes are saying, Not quite yet;
       Thy lips are saying, I'll say when.
Please overlook thy servant's presumption;
       please give him strength to satisfy thee
if satisfaction be thy will;
       if satisfying thee be possible.
Theology here gets kind of tricky,
       and thy servant is no theologian.
If he has aught that can serve thee,
       press it quickly into service.
If he runs out of time and space,
       bless the one who takes his place!

Zeal for thee dyes the day
        and steeps my dreams at night!
Zeal for thee tinctures my nerves
        and flavors all my sight!
Even when zeal takes a short break
        and we do nothing but rest,
how could someone feel alone
        lying next to thy hipbone?
Better than ginseng promotes greater bloodflow,
        better than honey or chocolate or oysters;
better than walnuts or rhino horn,
        gratitude inflames the soul!
Fairest Pharmacist, give me the dose
        according to thy prescription.
Though it be too much for me,
        let me risk the inflammation!

— III —

GREEN ZEBRA

Live in each season as it passes; breathe the air, drink the drink,
taste the fruit, and resign yourself to the influences of each.
—HDT

Help, Theophrastus,
or you, lewd Linnaeus,
with classes for plants and Sexual System

that borders on porn, "nine men in the chamber
of only one bride" sounds pretty wild
and might keep her happy, that passel of stamens
for only one pistil,
                    but where is the wild
found anymore, what's the vicinity
that hasn't been tilled by husbandry wholly
to nothing but cult, -ivated, -ivar;
                              take Adoration,
cocktail hybrid, or flat-globe Celebrity
or even Enchantment, all engineered
one way or another,
                    while here we were thinking,
when madly monandrous
                        and mounted like wolves
howling full moon beyond the tame pale,
we had evaded human improvement,
                              only to find
in ancient love manuals
                    we might as well be
a Cherokee Purple, another Big Rainbow,

or this zingy beauty with flavorful flesh
striped green and yellow.

ACCIDENTAL

Stowaway from Singapore,
no papers, no passport,
surname unknown,

Short-tailed Babbler, Japanese White-eye,
Orange-bellied Flowerpecker,

whoever you are, passing passerine,
drawn to perch on a lifeboat winch
by some crumb or flash of earring

as tugs yank the ship out into channel
and two days later, in South China Sea,

you're stuck too, nowhere to flee
from here to horizon, as shown by forays

of fluttering panic out over waves
and back before drowning,

little prisoner, condemned to be
transported to a dirtier city,

or if you hang on and cross all the way,
Black-throated Laughing Thrush
or whatever your name is,

a snack for hawks in the U.S.A.

JUICY GOSSIP

Avowedly the avocado's
partially autogamous

and would survive in solitude
playfully self-pollinating

its own receptive stigma
if only its small flowers,

pale-green, yellow-green
in racemes near the branch tips,

could open up concurrently
hermaphroditic organs

rather than flip-flop, hers today,
his tomorrow, but fruitfully the avocado

arrived from central Mexico
in two varieties, on different schedules,

so the trick, again, is simply to look
for one tree's mate at some remove

and there it stands, across the street,
orange-edged foliage of its peak

cresting the roof of another house,
beaming from another yard

its steady seed on wind or wing.

PERHAPS ONE SABBATH

Perhaps one Sabbath wasn't enough.
However holy or faithfully kept.
Perhaps restoration takes some people longer.
Even the ones not saving animals.
Perhaps busy Noah's main job description
Wasn't solely to make sure of specimens
Sufficient for mating and offering up
Clean versions of on the very first altar,
See Leviticus, chapter eleven, unknown to Noah
But coming soon and nothing compared
To chapter eighteen. Perhaps father Lamech
Spoke more truly than he could have known
When naming a son for relief he would bring
Once puddles had dried, vineyard took root
And pushed out its fruit, fermented by Noah,
hard-working patriarch and pioneer drunk
who after the Ark no one can blame
for giving us Sabbath at last in a glass.

HE CHOSE MINNESOTA

HDT, 1861

March fourth he ventured out
strolling along the Boston road
to bluebird burble, early that year,
sheltered by hill and out of all patience

with the state of the country, the State itself,
with statesmen in general, especially the president
sworn in that day. Mystic memory?
It made him sicker.

A shut-in at mid-month, thanks to last snows,
but come early April he set out inspecting
the scope of spring flood, unusually sensitive
to usual cold.
          Perhaps the West Indies,
his doctor suggested, but too muggy there
and Europe too costly, so he chose Minnesota
to try the dry air,
                  found for companion young Horace Mann
(two turned him down), and made out a checklist,
methodical as ever, carpet-bag, umbrella,
waist coat and plant book, writing paper, blotting paper,
pencils and shoestring, United States map,
drawers and best pants, socks, shirts, and jackknife,
watch and his ticket, needles, thread, pins,
warm cap and stamps, compass and spy glass,
microscope, medicine, seventy-eight dollars
in his left pocket, sixty in right,
forty in bosom.
          They left May eleventh,
the Sage having called to wish them good-bye,

provide introductions to friends on the way.
Already by Albany he felt pretty tired,
and someone in Chicago noted his voice,

"low but still sweet in tones and inflections,
though the organs, revolting, were wasting away
as he paused, now and then, to await the right word
or to master the trouble afflicting his chest,
but when he was through the sentence was perfect,
lacking in nothing; I read his books now
and don't hear my own voice but his from that day."

Aboard the *Itasca,* Mississippi at last,
he saw an encampment, "Dacotah-shaped wigwams,"
and arrived at St. Paul in a spring warming spell.
Nine days he botanized, sighted three species
of prairie gophers, fascinating, and watched volunteers
at Fort Snelling drilling.
                              Young Mann thought him better,
appetite good, coughing fits fewer, complaint of the bowels,
a gift of Chicago, finally abated.
                              Despite huge mosquitoes
he swam in the lakes and succeeded in plucking
for his herbarium one withered sample
of native crab apple, first seen from the train
as they crossed Michigan, elusive ever since,
until he feared missing it.
                              Why worry now?
Trip up the river, meeting Chief Little Crow,
buying Sioux snowshoes as useful souvenirs,
futile, all futile. The trip was a failure;
he knew it first.

Back home in the village,
late July now, he read in the paper
reports of his health with those of Bull Run.
Last journal entries describe a new kitten,
as perfectly protected by instincts in infancy
as by any wisdom "an old man can be."

Mann entered Harvard, majored in botany,
and groomed from the start would soon be the chair
but died, twenty-four, from consumption acquired,
the gossip would have it, on their trip west,

the only one made beyond Alleghenies
by his first mentor, if not the best.

AN ETHER PURER

Whenever a man hears it, he is young.
—HDT

Full Buck Moon come and gone,
or Thunder Moon, call it either,
the singing intensifies just before sunrise,

neither aubade—had he got laid,
he wouldn't be singing—nor serenade
because it's not evening,
               jet lag perhaps,
some other time zone calling his shots,
or maybe a loner late in the season
has to switch tactics,
               quit the high perches
away in safe woods to zero in low
up close to the window
               or end up a wallflower,
no genes transmitted, let alone lonely,
cicadas and dog days rubbing it in,

his failure to mate, despite the best song,
spun by this listener, solo and celibate,
into a triumph that refuses to please

a hard-to-get tease while singing deeper stuff
lasting all summer for sheer love of tune
designed to amuse
            the singer alone.
                  That's quite a lot
to load on a wood thrush,
             even in a journal entry,
July '52 included two moons, respectively full

first day and last,
                       5th was a Monday
so Sunday was tough, both Sabbath and 4th
piling it on,
             small wonder he heard
in the notes of the bird—avian amateurs
don't quote this part—
                   relief for the slave
in the house of his luxury,
                    relief for the inmate
of one's lowest thoughts.

WOE TO US HYPOCRITES

Hemingway's fantasy
of days when we're free
to shoot whom we please
hasn't got a chance
luckily for us
who trust we're the marksmen
and never the targets
so when you come home
from drudging through Monday
to news an old enemy,
nasty-cuss nemesis,
had open-heart surgery,
don't whoop and cheer,
just send him a card,
maybe some mums,
that dish of green beans
you've nearly perfected,
garlic, hot chili oil,
and bow to *hypocrisy*
for keeping the peace
with smiling mimesis
in spite of the anger
for which we're still liable
to judgment and fire;
there must be a reason
it's a translator's freebie,
a piece of the Greek
that's English to us.

GRANNY WAS AN ANGELFISH

*As for me, I collect pets: young girls—girls from ten to sixteen years old; girls who
are pretty and sweet and naïve and innocent—dear young creatures to whom
life is a perfect joy and to whom it has brought no wounds, no bitterness, and few
tears. My collection consists of gems of the first water.*

—AUTOBIOGRAPHY OF MARK TWAIN, *dictated February 12, 1908*

But she was only five when she joined,
Four months later, the Club with her sister,
Louise, fourteen, and Dorothy Harvey,
The Colonel's daughter, for cards on the terrace
His first week there, the villa then called
Innocence at Home. It didn't stick.
Summer solstice and Livy gone,
Terror harrowed his hours alone,
A neighbor wrote, taking the photo
Of four at the table intent on their hands,
Frocked older girls in big wicker chairs,
Same as their host in snowy flannels
With boiling white hair while little Joy,
Black bow in hers, dangled small feet
Over an iron one.
               Hard to believe
She mastered canasta or took to billiards
Or excelled at charades, but Angelfish pin
Clipped to her collar, she liked to ride
Down to the village with him in the car,
Debating the woods: Those, he said,
Are elephant woods. No they're not,
They're fairy woods, the fairies are there,
But we can't see them because they wear cloaks
That make them invisible. Oh, he said,
Sometimes I wish I had one of those;
I had one once, but it's worn out.

CUT AND PASTE

If spirit whispers *Roll your own gospel,* who's to gainsay
cutting and pasting, Jefferson's life of Jesus for instance
delivers the kid, snips off his foreskin with eyelids shut tight
on star and magi, sore afraid shepherds, angels on high,
whatever's supernatural need not apply, no job for John
until the Last Supper, washing up feet, having served first
nothing comestible, nothing fermented, so much for supper,
much less remembrance, as for resurrection, what are you,
kidding, roll up the stone and that's all she wrote,
though Mr. Monticello keenly liked precepts, stories with morals
mostly from Matthew, lots of Luke too, and the comment on John
it turns out is wrong, he got the nod for cleansing the temple,
his woman caught cheating survived expurgation, big surprise there,
as did the teaching that being born blind's no proof of sin,
good thing for us, cutting and pasting's a natural process
of natural selection, who can do otherwise, we can't stick in all
the laughable fractions we even see, but cutting and pasting
may deepen blindness, taste self-perpetuating handcuff itself,
got to paste in some challenges too, censor the healings
you overlook the overlook and don't forget miracle
rhymes with empirical, he said it best, left to herself
truth'll do fine, nothing to fear from apparent confliction,
strike things together you might get a spark, maybe the one
you've long been awaiting, chant the Lord's Prayer
in Luke's version, fine, in Greek if you like, or Latin or French,
each column glued beside the King's English, but then follow up
with something unlikely, let's push the statute, let's worship freely,
Jaya Ganesha or the Tryambakam, *mrityor mukshiya,* free us from death
as a gourd from its stem, or worship like a Miwok climbing up through
the tonsure of treeline in springtime Yosemite, unknown by Jefferson,
hadn't been wrested from Mexico yet, then coming down
from altitude solitude, thin air's high chill, to granite dome faces
tear-stained with snowmelt, it's up to you, you get to choose
whether to include, whether omit, Yosemite meant killers.

Damn your bare feet. Pierced nose.
Your baby's gold earrings. Bad cough. Big eyes.
Damn all your sisters in boisterous saris.
Your mother, your grandmother, each with her hand out.
Damn the hot street. And damn your quick mind.
This? *Mooku.* English? *Nose.*
This? *Vaay.* English? *Mouth.*
Dark arm, light arm, what could be funnier
than mismatching pigment: such potable laughter.
English? *I love you.* Damn your calling after
I love you I love you. And double-damn home
in the land of safe water with potency sabotaged
to care who's in first. Who's all the rage.

FOREIGN BODY

Snake bite, lightning strike,
one more day-shift in the ER:
how to snap the old gal's hip
back in place; how to get the wasp-stung lip
smaller than a hockey puck.
Read in his palm the broken beer bottle
fifteen stitches later; fly again across an ocean
on the blood clot in her calf.
But this tough glitch,
in from out where there's no need
to lock one's doors against a burglar,
let us let the surgeon handle
abdominal pain and x-ray explained
*I slipped on a stair and landed by chance
just the wrong way and now it's stuck there,*
a private flashlight, no longer hidden
though ready to shine with each new step,
at home, at work, Sunday at church,
on delicate tissue, difficult pleasure.

Call me Neanderthal   and that's a mean putdown
but even if he lacked a chin   the simple fact
he invented the hand axe   and then turned that hand
to bury his dead   means he had something
going on inside him   because if disgusted
by bad smell alone   he could have just thrown
the corpse down a gorge   an easier option
than digging up ground   hardened by ice age
and piling up stones   atop a fresh grave
someone merely crude   and nothing but boorish
wouldn't take such care   but even more impressive
he performed this chore   gagging with sadness
for sixty thousand years   before art came along
and all its squirmy doodlers   with a fetish for figures
like creative Cro-Magnon   who couldn't kill a mammoth
without running home   and replaying the kill
all over his cave   so millennia later
thirty or forty   somewhere in France
here we are oohing   over a marvel
that led to idolatry   and a second commandment
prohibiting images   which only estrange us
from both the concrete   and the silent abstract
and forget it once writing   also arose
to make it impossible   to kill that same mammoth
without sticky style   estranging us again
as though basic mammoth-killing   needed estranging
so call me Neanderthal   and you can be Cro-Magnon
with your pretty artful chin   and your arty chin music.

CASSEROLE FOR THE BEREAVED

Please, it's nothing. Just what there was
lying around: the yellow breastplate
of a painted turtle, that trickster basking
these millions of years;

black cohosh flowers in tight white clusters,
eye-high stem, the sweet, fetid smell
attractive to gnats, whether the extracts
sedate or not;

and last the brash chatter of two brown thrashers
defending nests with golden eyes
and three thousand songs in the repertoire.

Already baked, so heat a low oven
of muggy weather and serve with a salad
of afternoon clouds. The least I could do.

PEACE AND QUIET

no escape
even in woods
rubs and scrapes
of bucks in rut
saplings snapped
and stubs all smeared
in eye-gland musk
followed by frantic
dot dot dot
down wet-leaved trail
those patches his rack
rips clean to dirt
gouged by tines
the fevered ellipses
defining a line
so a doe distressed
by urgent estrus
can hunt him at dusk

THE QING CONQUEST STIRRED
LOYALIST PASSIONS

in Chen Zilong (1608–47) and Liu Shi (1618–64). The two poets
were lovers, but she later married another poet, Qian Qianyi
(1582–1664), who left his wife for her.

Because one can rhyme
with ease in Chinese
there have to be rules
making things harder.
They broke none of these.
Nor did appeasing
and pleasing themselves
eclipse all the rest.

True, they drank too much
tiger bone wine once
and lay in a cart
beneath a thin moon
fondling freely
according to code,
Four Tones and Eight Faults,
striving to balance

level with *rising,*
also *departing,*
two poets at work,
off-duty never,
even his patterns
of fingering touch
pentasyllabic,
except in Chinese

no word means *poet,*
since why have a word
for what none is not?
Highest distinction,
Maker or Master,
comes from embracing
more challenging rules,
not just avoiding

the *entering* tone
in some positions
of disciplined lines.
Can saints of restraint
add a new timbre
by how they abstain
beneath a thin moon,
though neither has waned?

What happened later
by the great fireplace,
the servants asleep
and she having slipped
silk from her shoulders?
Would it then differ,
pain of refraining,
because of his age?

Thirty-six winters
he had for cooling
before she smelled spring.
She took Buddhist vows
when they accused him.

The yellow gingko
impeding north wind
continued to bear

the childhood tree house
she hid herself in,
a geisha at play
when he had found her,
thunderstorm coming,
to undo her sash
and soothe her youth there.
They died the same year.

*Note: In traditional Chinese lyric poetry of the Southern Dynasties,
prosody became codified according to the "Four Tones and Eight
Faults." The four tones were called level, rising, departing, and
entering, and the eight faults resulted from repeating tones or sounds
in certain positions of a given line or rhyming couplet.*

"I AM IN IRELAND NOW"

G. M. Hopkins

Water to wine, all very fine, but water from St. James's Wells,
roasted barley, female hops, and yeast descended from the founder's time
and you've got Guinness, and Guinness is good for you.
Just ask the toucan. The Guinnesses, too. Brewers, true,
but also philanthropists, Benjamin re-doing St. Patrick's Cathedral,
so Swift can lie there snug with Stella, and building on St. Stephen's Green,
southern side, the Iveagh House (pronounce it like the climbing vine)
complete with gardens, also restored, left to Edward, third-born son,
whose children used to play croquet there, perhaps their wickets
recklessly close to Nike fountains, a pair of them wingèd
and not over-dressed, as the priest looked on, south and down
from his second-floor window (we'd say third) on sunny fun
beer can buy. There's plenty of evidence he was depressed,
take your pick of things he wrote there, desk and chair, fitful bed,
but what a great view of Guinness's gardens, and if Belgian Trappists
can savor their ale, why can't a Jesuit break from his Greek
and head to the pub for one quiet pint? Guinness for strength.
It must have been something; how else could he end,
"I am so happy, I am so happy, I loved my life"?

To each family its own pattern.
Diamond, O'Donnell. Honeycomb, Mullin.
Basket stitch, for plentiful catch, Flaherty, always hopeful.
And to each pattern its own fingers
knitting through her afternoon evenings, evil weather,
rising fear of rising waves, a widowing world
of fish and wind narrowed to an extra needle,
a local texture, permutations, handed down
by village wives, spinster aunts, one-cable serpentine,
two-cable rope, three for a plait, princess braid, Saxon braid
ending in a stiff ribbed cuff. To each cuff
gestures and motions, hauling a line, lifting a glass,
miming a cross, sometimes in a low thatched house
climbing up to stroke a cheek. Or to strike it.
Whatever the pattern, the wearer's initials
finish off the bottom edge
should islanding ocean ever wash up
some faceless thing in need of a name.

CRASH COURSE

Lower Ninth Ward, One Year after Hurricane Katrina

Even if polyglot, who speaks fluently
the tongue of ruin that's mother here,
where lavish grasses fringe the eaves
of a garbled roof in purple wildbloom,
or masters the grammar of local dialect,
its syntax of twisted stop sign stanchions
and agreement of the sudden flood-burst,
understood referent now receded
from front steps marking a house erased,
with telephone poles still adjectival,
street after street after tenantless street,
leaning away from the ruptured levee?

CRISIS HOTLINE

What a surprise
to find the creek noise
in fact arises from the opposite ridge
where a new band of rain inching eastward
already natters on long-distance leaves
though local sky above stays dry

but what a surprise
like that should mean
to someone saying she can't see a reason
to get out of bed or go on living
would take some explaining
which might not work.

ROMMEL'S OPTION

Good-byes come in many sizes.
There's see you later, see you soon,
take a hike, and don't you dare
show that face near here again.

But let's agree that having to say,
one October Saturday, Lucie *Meine Liebste,*
these two gentlemen, here from Berlin,
bring to Herrlingen choice and their promise

you and Manfred have freedom to live
as pensioned widow and hero's son
if I bite this cyanide
differs from the rest of them.

DARK SOCIAL

Saturday morning daredevil foreplay,
red-shouldered courtship spiral display
by monogamous mates, first in wide loops
above the frayed trees, then into stunt dives
urge pulls them out of a few yards away
just before impact under leaf canopy
or where one would be if April this year
quit casting cold spells, frigid air layer
close to the ground refracting intenser
hush-threshing wing-blades
venting a need for breeding again
and nothing beyond their twin immolation
without an apostle to bear distant witness,
nary a follower clicking and liking.

MATED FOR LIFE

As though a goose alone on the pond

or make it a gander passersby take

for solo rogue maverick afloat on composure,

detachment, free-standing, easy to hate

an avian Emerson whose celibate wake

of self-assured ripples ruffles our orgy,

our frenzy, promiscuous, of surface connections,

how dare he, really, pretend to transcend us

until the light dims on dusky discovery

up in the woods above the far bank

of goose down with feathers a little too

scattered for nesting while lying beside,

this part's not fun but what can you do,

coyote leavings to honk at in goose tongue

for wailing and howling as Pink Moon appears

to sob on his vigil, his other lone wake.

LAST TIME IN PERSON

Luke 9:29

It's a sign
she's making for face
after for change

she flips her clenched fists
next flashing quick
sun and then shine

clothing becoming
white plus the dazzle
she does very well

with hand a small zigzag
downwardly bolting
figure for fulgurate

all signs she makes
Sunday for a couple
of white-headed guys

down front in a pew
two from the pulpit
she has her back to

never once glancing
up toward the balcony
with the best view

for seeing Our Father
in silent duet
before the guys turn

to help us learn passing
the peace across distance

lusciously touching.

CPSIA information can be obtained
at www.ICGtesting.com
Printed in the USA
LVHW101100240822
726712LV00001B/15